WORSHIP SONGS FROM AUSTRALIA

25 Easy-to-play arrangements
for keyboard and guitar

WORSHIP SONGS FROM AUSTRALIA

25 Easy-to-play arrangements
for keyboard and guitar

Kevin Mayhew

We hope you enjoy the music in this book. Further copies are available from your local music shop or Christian bookshop.

In case of difficulty, please contact the publisher direct by writing to:

The Sales Department
KEVIN MAYHEW LTD
Buxhall
Stowmarket
Suffolk IP14 3BW

Phone 01449 737978
Fax 01449 737834
E-mail info@kevinmayhewltd.com

Please ask for our complete catalogue of outstanding Church Music.

First published in Great Britain in 1999 by Kevin Mayhew Ltd.

© Copyright 1999 Kevin Mayhew Ltd.

ISBN 1 84003 487 4
ISMN M 57004 642 3
Catalogue No: 1450163

0 1 2 3 4 5 6 7 8 9

Front cover illustration by Karen Perrins
Cover design by Jaquetta Sergeant

Music arrangements by Keith Stent
Music Editor/Setter: Geoffrey Moore
Proofreader: Rachel Judd

Printed and bound in Great Britain

Index

	Song number
All things are possible	1
Almighty God, My Redeemer	1
And that my soul knows very well	24
Before the world began	2
Father of creation	22
Father of life, draw me closer	3
Glory to the King of kings	4
I believe the promise	5
I belong to you	17
I bow my knee	6
I give you my heart	19
I know it	7
I'll love you more	6
I'm so secure	8
In your hands	8
I've found a friend	9
I will run to you	25
Jesus, God's righteousness revealed	10
Jesus, lover of my soul	11
Jesus, what a beautiful name	12
Jesus, you're all I need	13
Joy in the Holy Ghost	9
Latter rain	20

Let the peace of God reign	3
Lord, I come to you	14
Lord, I give my life to you	15
My Jesus, my Saviour	16
Now is the time	21
Open arms	17
Power of your love	14
Shout to the Lord	16
So you would come	10
Surrender	15
The power and the glory	18
This grace is mine	18
This is my desire	19
This is the hour	20
This kingdom	10
This love	21
Touching heaven, changing earth	23
We come into your presence	22
We will seek your face	23
You make your face to shine on me	24
Your eye is on the sparrow	25

Important Copyright Information

The Publishers wish to express their gratitude to the copyright owners who have granted permission to include their copyright material in this book. Full details are clearly indicated on the respective pages.

The **words** of the songs in this publication are covered by a **Church Copyright Licence** which allows local church reproduction on overhead projector acetates, in service bulletins, songsheets, audio/visual recording and other formats.

The **music** in this book is covered by the newly introduced 'add-on' **Music Reproduction Licence** issued by CCL (Europe) Ltd and you may photocopy the music and words of the songs in this book provided:

You hold a current Music Reproduction Licence from CCL (Europe) Ltd.

The copyright owner of the hymn or song you intend to photocopy is included in the Authorised Catalogue List which comes with your Music Reproduction Licence.

Full details of both the Church Copyright Licence and the additional Music Reproduction Licence are available from:

Christian Copyright Licensing (Europe) Ltd, PO Box 1339, Eastbourne, East Sussex, BN21 4YF. Tel: 01323 417711, fax: 01323 417722, e-mail: info@ccli.com, web: www.ccli.com

Please note, all texts and music in this book are protected by copyright and if you do not possess a licence from CCL (Europe) Ltd, they may not be reproduced in any way for sale or private use without the consent of the copyright owner.

1 Almighty God, my Redeemer
(All things are possible)
Darlene Zschech

Al-migh-ty God, my Re-deem-er, my hid-ing-place, my safe re-fuge, no o-ther name like Je-sus, no pow'r can stand a-gainst you. my Lord, and my sal-va-tion. Your praise is al-ways on my lips, your word is liv-ing in my heart

My feet are plant-ed on this rock and I will not be sha-ken. My hope, it comes from you a-lone, my Lord, and my sal-va-tion. You fill my life with grea-ter joy, yes, I de-light my-self in you and I will praise

© Copyright 1997 Darlene Zschech/Hillsong Music Australia/Kingsway's Thankyou Music,
P.O. Box 75, Eastbourne, East Sussex, BN23 6NW, UK. Used by permission.

you with a new song, my soul will bless you, Lord.

2. *D.C.* *4.*
you, Lord.   you, Lord. When I am weak, you make me strong.

When I'm poor, I know I'm rich, for in the pow-er of your name

all things are pos - si - ble,   all things are pos - si - ble,

all things are pos - si - ble,   all things are pos - si - ble.

2 Before the world began
(So you would come)

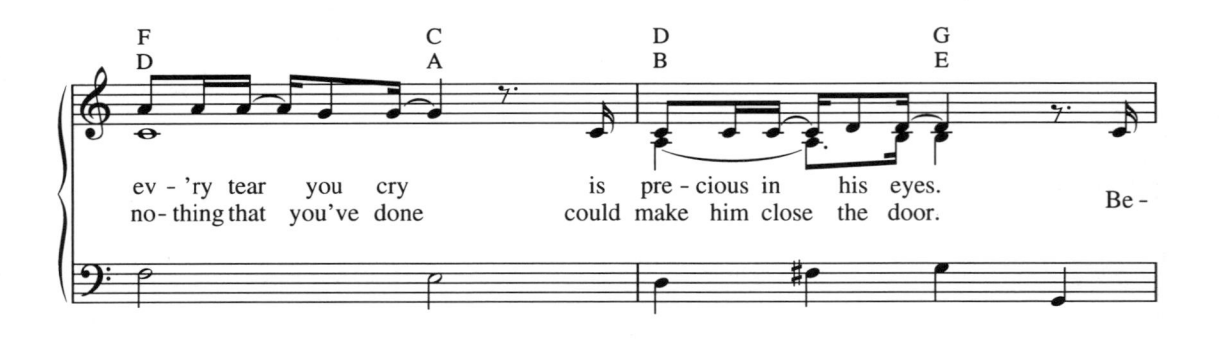

Russell Fragar

Capo 3

Be-fore the world be-gan you were on his mind, and ev-'ry tear you cry is pre-cious in his eyes.
No-thing you can do could make him love you more, and no-thing that you've done could make him close the door.

Be-cause of his great love, he gave his on-ly Son; ev-'ry-thing was done so you would come.

© Copyright 1996 Russell Fragar/Hillsong Music Australia/Kingsway's Thankyou Music,
P.O. Box 75, Eastbourne, East Sussex, BN23 6NW, UK. Used by permission.

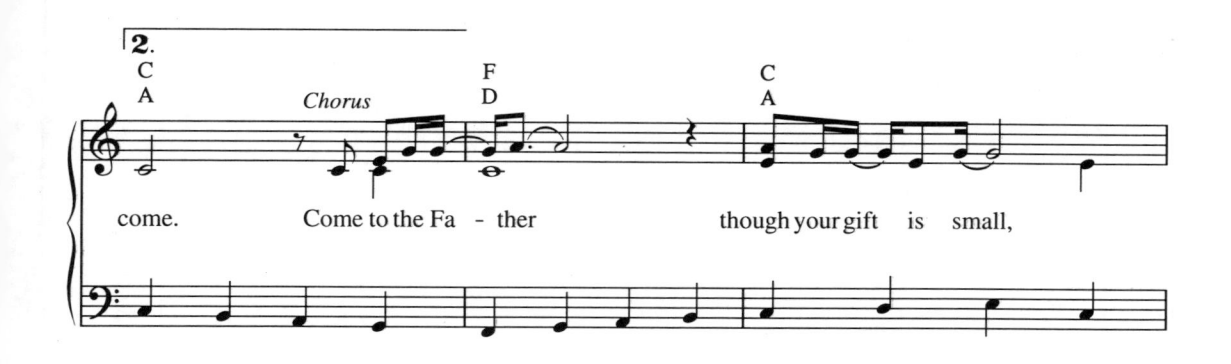

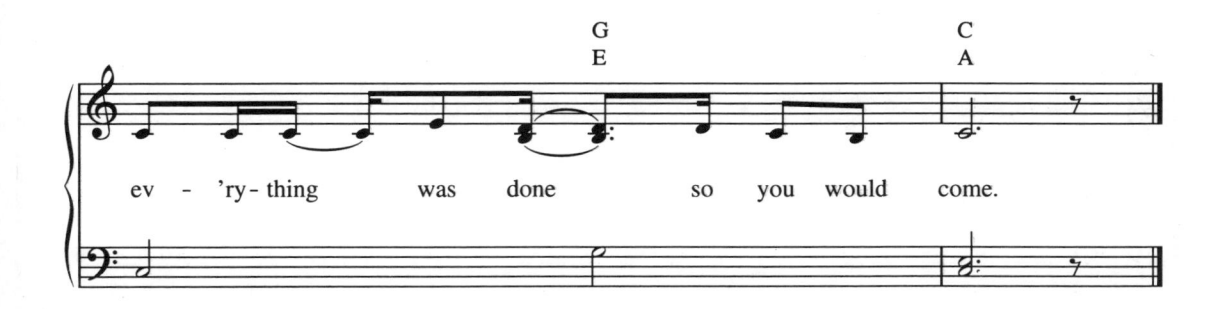

2.

come. Come to the Fa - ther though your gift is small, broken hearts, broken lives, he will take them all. The power of the Word, the power of his blood, ev-'ry-thing was done so you would come.

3 Father of life, draw me closer
(Let the peace of God reign)

Darlene Zschech

Fa - ther of life   draw me clo - ser,   Lord, my heart is set on
O   Ho - ly Spi - rit, Lord, my com - fort,   strength - en me, hold my

you.   let me run the race of time   with your
head   up high;   and I'll stand up - on your truth,   bring - ing

life en - fold - ing mine   and let the peace   of God,   let it reign.
glo - ry un - to you,

reign.   O Lord, I hun - ger for   more of you,

© Copyright 1995 Darlene Zschech/Hillsong Music Australia/Kingsway's Thankyou Music,
P.O. Box 75, Eastbourne, East Sussex, BN23 6NW, UK. Used by permission.

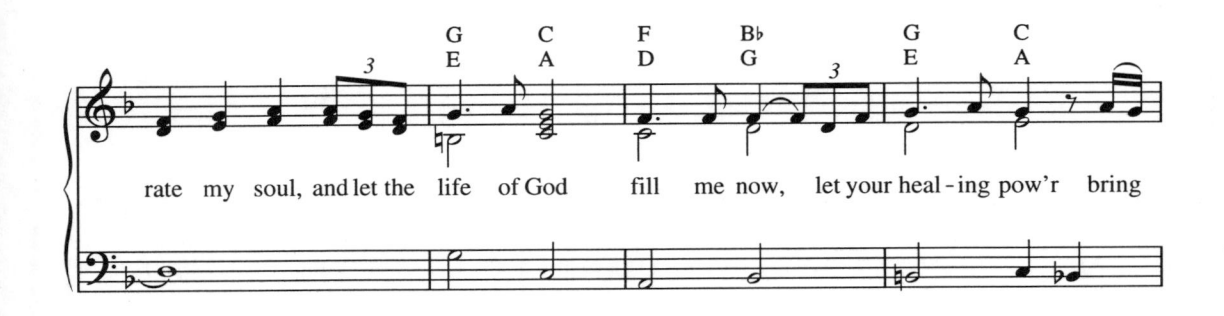

rise up with-in me, let me know your truth. O Ho-ly Spi - rit, sa-tu-rate my soul, and let the life of God fill me now, let your heal-ing pow'r bring life and make me whole and let the peace of God, let it reign.

4 Glory to the King of kings

Geoff Bullock

Chorus

Glory to the King of kings!
Majesty, pow'r and strength to the Lord of lords!

1. Holy One, all creation crowns you King of kings.
   Holy One, King of kings, Lord of lords, Holy One.

2. Jesus, Lord, with eyes unveiled we will see your throne.
   Jesus, Prince of Peace, Son of God, Emmanuel.

© Copyright 1992 Word/Maranatha! Music. Administered by CopyCare, P.O. Box 77, Hailsham, East Sussex, BN27 3EF, UK. (music@copycare.com). Used by permission.

2.

Glo - ry to the King of kings! Ma - jes - ty, pow'r and strength to the Lord of lords, pow'r and strength to the Lord of lords, pow'r and strength to the Lord of lords.

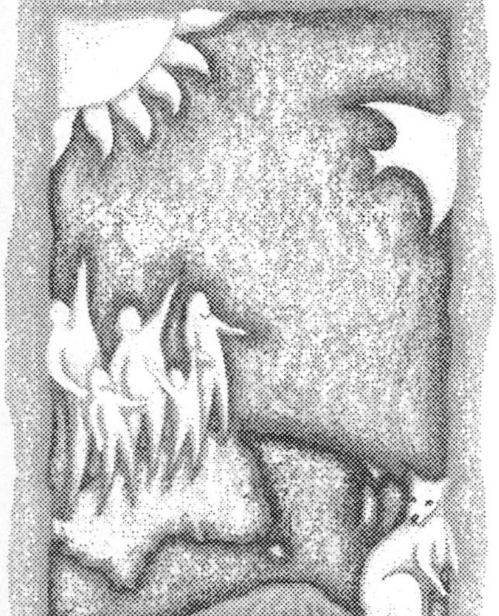

5 I believe the promise

Russell Fragar

Capo 3

1. I believe the promise about the visions and the dreams that the Holy Spirit will be poured out and his power will be seen. Well, the time is now and the place is here and his people have come in faith; there's a mighty sound and a torch of fire when we're gathered in one place.

© Copyright 1995 Russell Fragar/Hillsong Music Australia/Kingsway's Thankyou Music,
P.O. Box 75, Eastbourne, East Sussex, BN23 6NW, UK. Used by permission.

I be-lieve that the pre-sence of God is here;
there's not one thing that can't be changed when the Spi-rit of God is near.
I be-lieve that the pre-sence of God is here
when two or three are ga-thered, when peo-ple rise in faith,

Last time to Coda

I be-lieve God ans-wers and his pre-sence is in this place.

1. D.C.

2.

Nothing in earth or heaven can stop the pow'r of God;
into our hand is given the call to take it on;
no ocean can contain it, no star can rise above;
into our hearts is given the pow'r of his love
presence is in this place.

D.S. al Coda — **CODA**

6 I bow my knee
(I'll love you more)

Rob and Debbie Eastwood

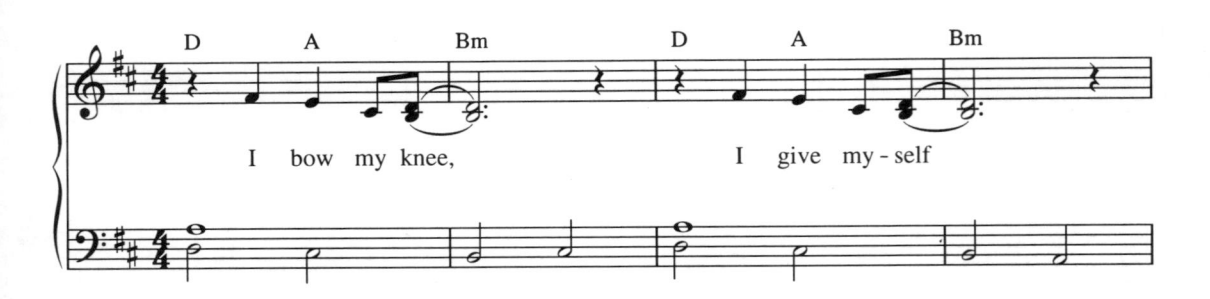

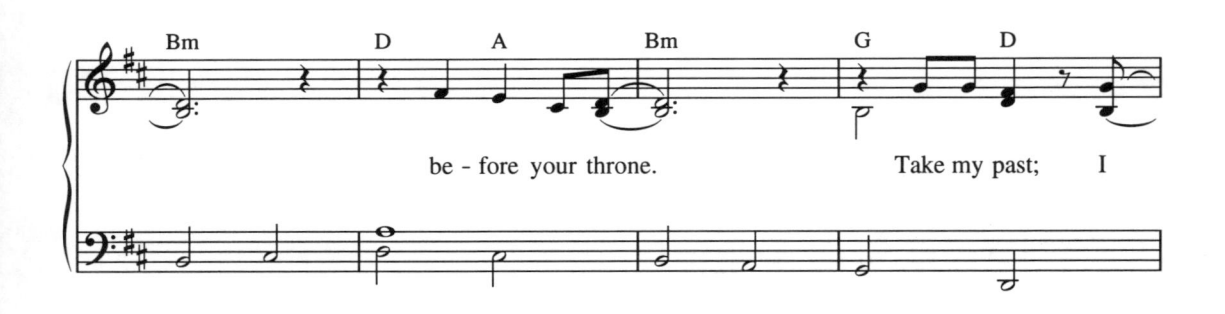

I bow my knee, I give my-self as a liv-ing sac-ri-fice for you. I lay me down be-fore your throne. Take my past; I will stand for you. Let your blood wash o-ver me,

© Copyright 1992 Debbie and Rob Eastwood/Hillsong Music Australia/Kingsway's Thankyou Music,
P.O. Box 75, Eastbourne, East Sussex, BN23 6NW, UK. Used by permission.

let your blood wash o - ver me; you have cleansed my heart and set my spi - rit free.

You are my Lord, I'll love you more, I'll fol - low you, no mat - ter when, no mat - ter where.

2nd time D.C.

Last time

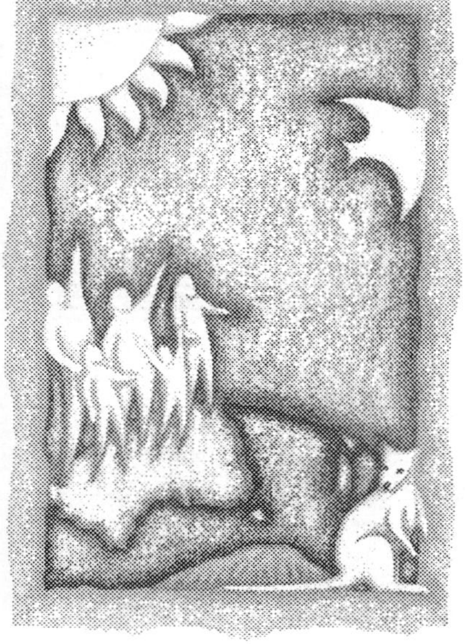

7 I know it

Darlene Zschech

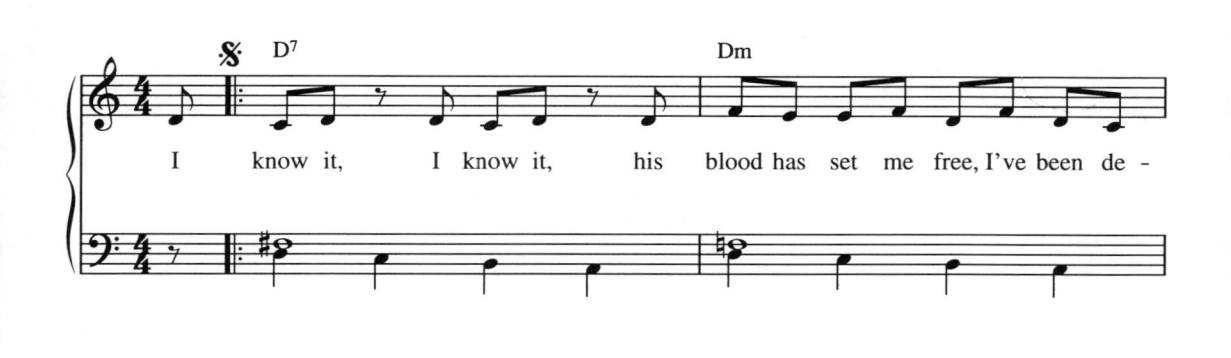

I know it, I know it, his blood has set me free, I've been delivered, forgiven, fear has got no hold on me. I'm set apart, not living life my own way, not holding back till I see him face to face because I know it, oh yes, I know it. I

© Copyright 1997 Darlene Zschech/Hillsong Music Australia/Kingsway's Thankyou Music,
P.O. Box 75, Eastbourne, East Sussex, BN23 6NW, UK. Used by permission.

know it. The blood of Je-sus has set me free! I free! free! There is heal-ing in the name of Je-sus, sal-va-tion in the name of Je-sus, for-give-ness in the name of Je-sus. I've ne-ver known it like I know it to-day; there is pow-er in the name of Je - sus, full-ness of joy I've found in Je - sus, strength in the name of Je - sus. I know it, I know it, oh, I've got to tell you that I

D.S. al Fine

8 I'm so secure
(In your hands)

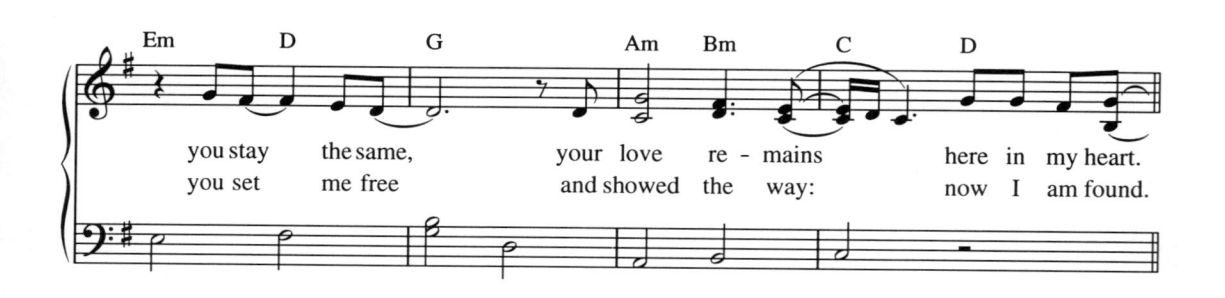

Reuben Morgan

1. I'm so secure, you're here with me;
   you stay the same, your love remains here in my heart.
2. You gave your life in your endless love,
   you set me free and showed the way: now I am found.

Chorus

So close I believe you're holding me now, in your hands I belong.
You'll never let me go. So close I believe you're holding me now,

© Copyright 1996 Reuben Morgan/Hillsong Music Australia/Kingsway's Thankyou Music,
P.O. Box 75, Eastbourne, East Sussex, BN23 6NW. Used by permission.

1.
To end
C G Am D Em D C Dsus4 G
D.C.
Fine
in your hands I be-long. You'll ne-ver let me go.
2.
C G C B7 Em D
All a-long, you were be-side me, e-ven when I could-n't tell.
C G C D
D.S. al Fine
Through the years you showed me more of you, more of you.

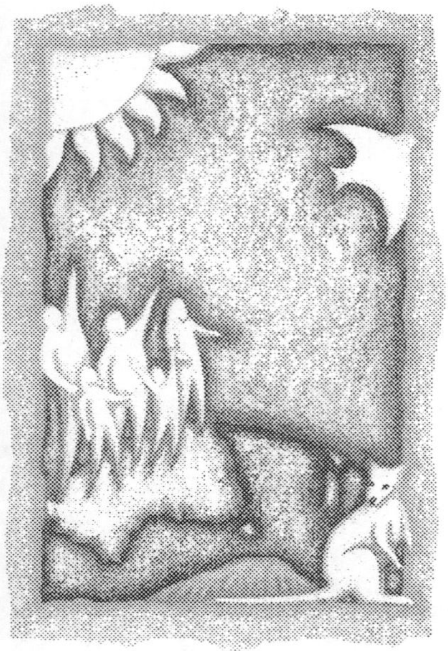

9 I've found a friend
(Joy in the Holy Ghost)

Russell Fragar

1. I've found a friend, O such a friend, he made my heart his home.
   Holy Spirit fills me up and I need him ev-'ry day
   for God himself is with me and I know I'm never alone.
   fire, faith and confidence and knowing what to say.
   I know all my tomorrows will be better than all my hopes;
   I gave my heart and all I am to the one who loves me most;
   we've got

© Copyright 1996 Russell Fragar/Hillsong Music Australia/Kingsway's Thankyou Music,
P.O. Box 75, Eastbourne, East Sussex, BN23 6NW, UK. Used by permission.

love! grace! peace and pow'r and joy in the Ho-ly Ghost.

Chorus
My God is ne-ver wrong and he makes time for me. It blew a-part my chains and set this sin-ner free. It's like a ri-ver and you'll ne-ver run it dry.

We've got pow - er o - ver fear and death and hearts filled up with joy. 2. The we've got love! grace! peace and pow'r and joy in the Ho-ly Ghost.

10 Jesus, God's righteousness revealed
(This kingdom)

Geoff Bullock

1. Jesus, God's righteousness revealed, the Son of Man, the Son of God, his kingdom comes. Jesus, redemption's sacrifice, now glorified, now justified, his kingdom

2. Jesus, the expression of God's love, the grace of God, the Word of God, revealed to us; Jesus, God's holiness displayed, his kingdom

© Copyright 1995 Word/Maranatha! Music. Administered by CopyCare,
P.O. Box 77, Hailsham, East Sussex, BN27 3EF, UK. (music@copycare.com). Used by permission.

comes. And this king-dom will know no end, and its glo-ry shall know no bounds, for the ma-jes-ty and pow-er of this king-dom's King has come, and this king-dom's reign, and this king-dom's rule, and this king-dom's pow-er and au-tho-ri-ty, Je-sus, God's right-eous-ness re-vealed.

11 Jesus, lover of my soul

John Ezzy, Daniel Grul and Stephen McPherson

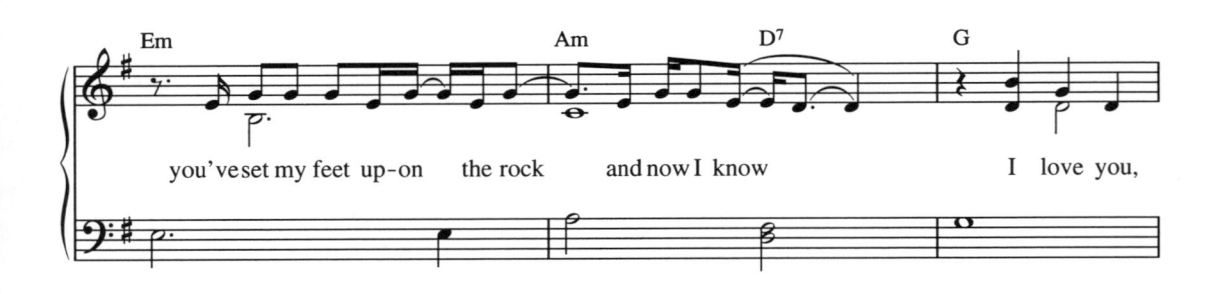

Je - sus, lov-er of my soul, Je - sus, I will
ne-ver let you go; you've ta-ken me from the mi - ry clay,
you've set my feet up-on the rock and now I know I love you,
I need you, though my world will fall, I'll ne-ver let you go.

© Copyright 1992 John Ezzy, Daniel Grul, Stephen McPherson/Hillsong Music Australia/
Kingsway's Thankyou Music, P.O. Box 75, Eastbourne, East Sussex, BN23 6NW, UK. Used by permission.

My Sa-viour, my clos-est friend, I will wor-ship you un-til the ve-ry end. til the ve-ry end.

12 Jesus, what a beautiful name

Tanya Riches

1. Je - sus, what a beau-ti-ful name. Son of God, Son of Man, Lamb that was slain. Joy and peace, strength and hope, grace that blows all fear a-way. Je - sus, what a beau-ti-ful name.

2. Je - sus, what a beau-ti-ful name. Truth re-vealed, my fu-ture sealed, healed my pain. Love and free-dom, life and warmth, grace that blows all fear a-way. Je - sus, what a beau-ti-ful name.

© Copyright 1995 Tanya Riches/Hillsong Music Australia/Kingsway's Thankyou Music,
P.O. Box 75, Eastbourne, East Sussex, BN23 6NW, UK. Used by permission.

name. 3. Je - sus, what a beau-ti-ful name.

Res-cued my soul, my strong-hold, lifts me from shame.

For-give-ness, se - cu - ri - ty, pow-er and love, grace that blows all

fear a-way. Je - sus, what a beau-ti-ful name.

13 Jesus, you're all I need

Darlene Zschech

Capo 3

Je-sus, you're all I need, you're all I need.
Now I give my life to you a-lone,
you are all I need, Je-sus, you're all I
need, you're all I need. Lord, you gave
your-self so I could live, you are all I need.

Fine

© Copyright 1997 Darlene Zschech/Hillsong Music Australia/Kingsway's Thankyou Music,
P.O. Box 75, Eastbourne, East Sussex, BN23 6NW, UK. Used by permission.

Oh, you pur-chased my sal-va-tion and wiped a-way my tears, now I drink your liv-ing wa-ters and I'll ne-ver thirst a-gain. For you a-lone are ho-ly, I'll wor-ship at your throne and you will reign for e-ver, ho-ly is the Lord.

D.C.

14 Lord, I come to you
(Power of your love)

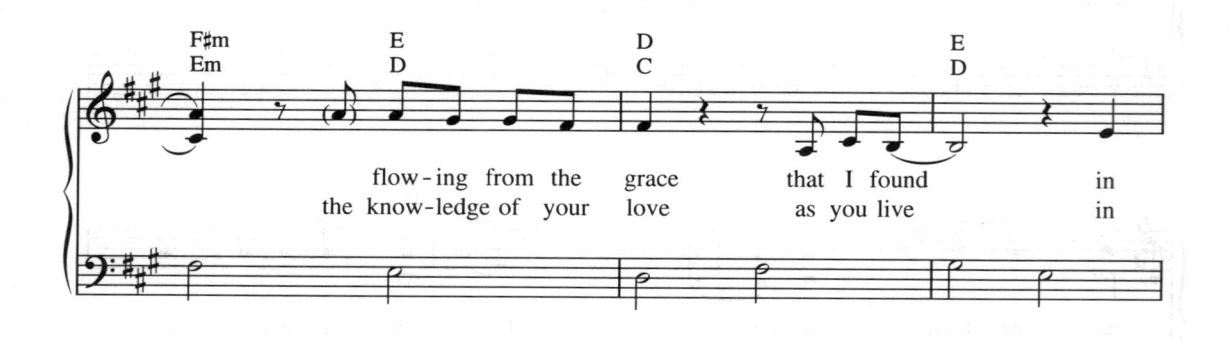

Geoff Bullock

1. Lord, I come to you, let my heart be changed, re-newed, flowing from the grace that I found in you.
2. Lord, un-veil my eyes, let me see you face to face, the knowledge of your love as you live in me.

And, Lord, I've come to know the weak-nes-ses I see in me will be stripped a-
Lord, re-new my mind as your will un-folds in my life, in liv-ing ev-'ry

© Copyright 1992 Word/Maranatha! Music. Administered by CopyCare,
P.O. Box 77, Hailsham, East Sussex, BN27 3EF, UK. (music@copycare.com). Used by permission.

way by the pow'r of your love.
day in the pow'r of your love.

Chorus

Hold me close, let your love sur-round me,

bring me near, draw me to your side; and

as I wait, I'll rise up like an ea - gle, and I will soar with you;

your Spi-rit leads me on in the pow'r of your love.

15 Lord, I give my life to you
(Surrender)

Geoff Bullock

1. Lord, I give my life to you, there's no-thing left to do, I sur-render.
   Lord, I bring my heart to you, your love can see me through, I surrender. And in bro-ken-ness and pain you help me love a-gain with the

2. give my dreams, my plans, ev-'ry-thing and all I am, I sur-render.
   And I bring my love for you, there's no-thing I can do, I surrender. As a liv-ing sa-cri-fice, you've come to give me life and the

© Copyright 1997 Watershed Productions/Kingsway's Thankyou Music,
P.O. Box 75, Eastbourne, East Sussex, BN23 6NW, UK. (UK only.) Used by permission.

grace that gent-ly heals my soul.
love that o-ver-whelms my soul. So I bring this heart, this life, the

trou-bles and the strife, I sur-ren - der. 2. Lord, I

Chorus

All that I am and e-ver hope to be

was planned be-fore my day of birth. Ev-'ry word and ev-'ry

thought, O my Lord, you know me well. 2. Lord, I

16 My Jesus, my Saviour
(Shout to the Lord)
Darlene Zschech

Growing in strength

My Jesus, my Saviour, Lord, there is none like you.
My comfort, my shelter, tower of refuge and strength,

All of my days I want to praise the wonders of your
let ev-'ry breath, all that I am,

mighty love. never cease to worship you.

Shout to the Lord, all the earth, let us sing power and majesty, praise
I sing for joy at the work of your hands. For ever I'll love you, for e-

© Copyright 1993 Darlene Zschech/Hillsong Music Australia/Kingsway's Thankyou Music,
P.O. Box 75, Eastbourne, East Sussex, BN23 6NW, UK. Used by permission.

to the King. Moun-tains bow down and the seas will roar at the
- ver I'll stand. No-thing com-pares to the pro-

sound of your name. - mise I have in you.

17 Open arms
(I belong to you)
Reuben Morgan

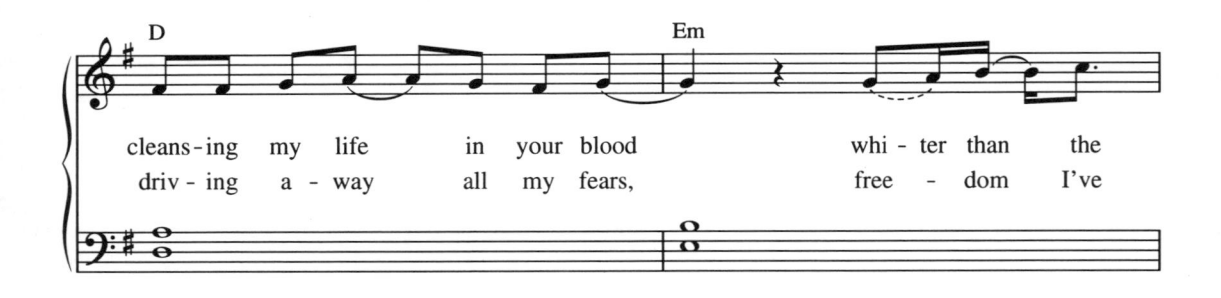

1. O-pen arms welcome me close to your heart,
and there I long to stay. Mercy falls,
cleansing my life in your blood, whiter than the snow.
I belong to you, Jesus, my first love.

2. Take my life, join me for ever with you;
make our hearts as one. Perfect love,
driving away all my fears, freedom I've found.
I belong to you, Jesus, my first love.

© Copyright 1997 Reuben Morgan/Hillsong Music Australia/Kingsway's Thankyou Music,
P.O. Box 75, Eastbourne, East Sussex, BN23 6NW, UK. Used by permission.

You're ev-'ry-thing I'm liv-ing for,
you're the joy I know, the trea-sure I hold dear;
I burn for you, my e-ter-nal love.

Je - sus, my e-ter - nal love.

D.S. al Fine

18 This grace is mine
(The power and the glory)
Geoff Bullock

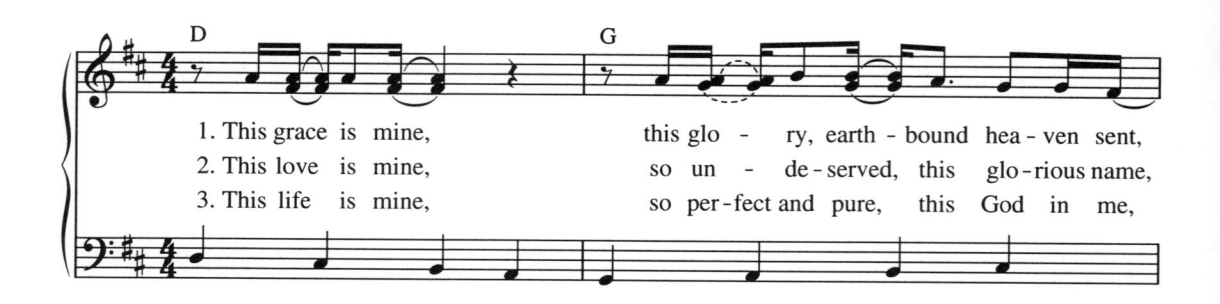

1. This grace is mine, this glo - ry, earth - bound hea - ven sent,
2. This love is mine, so un - de - served, this glo - rious name,
3. This life is mine, so per - fect and pure, this God in me,

this plan di - vine, this life, this light that breaks my night,
this Son, this God, this life, this death, this vic - t'ry won,
this glo - rious hope from earth to hea - ven, death to life,

the Spi - rit of God hea - ven falls like a dove to my heart.
for - give - ness has flowed and this grace that is mine finds my heart.
this fu - ture as - sured and se - cured by this love in my heart.

To verse 2 | 2, 3.

Chorus

The

© Copyright 1994 Word/Maranatha! Music. Administered by CopyCare,
P.O. Box 77, Hailsham, East Sussex, BN27 3EF, UK. (music@copycare.com). Used by permission.

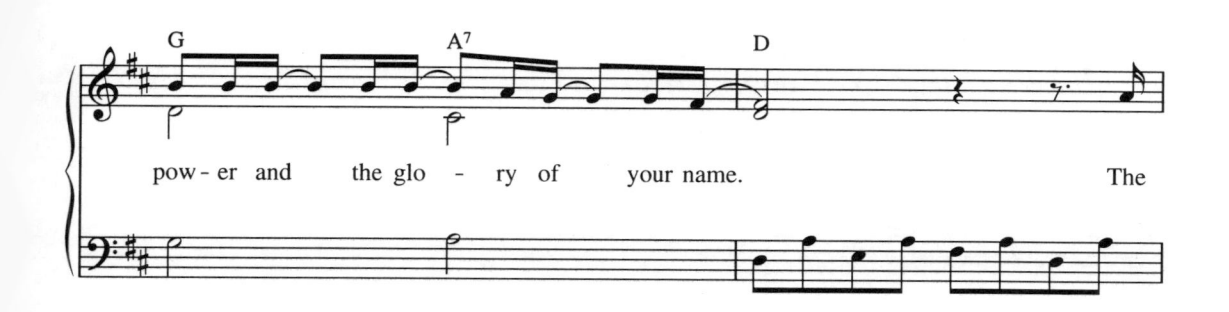

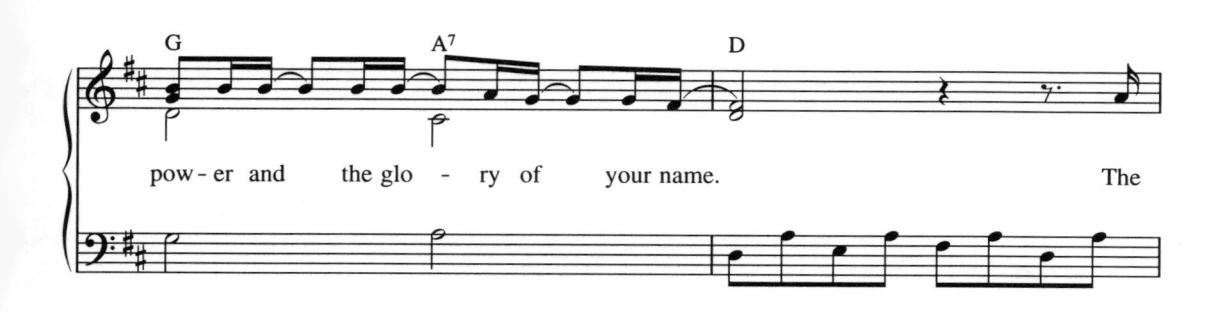

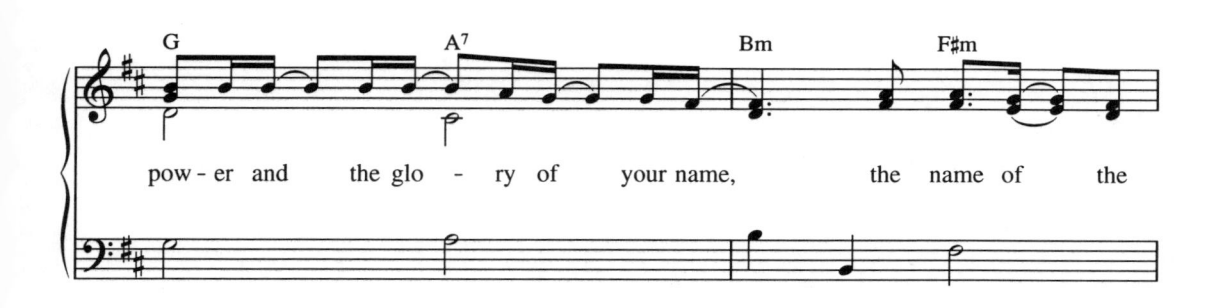

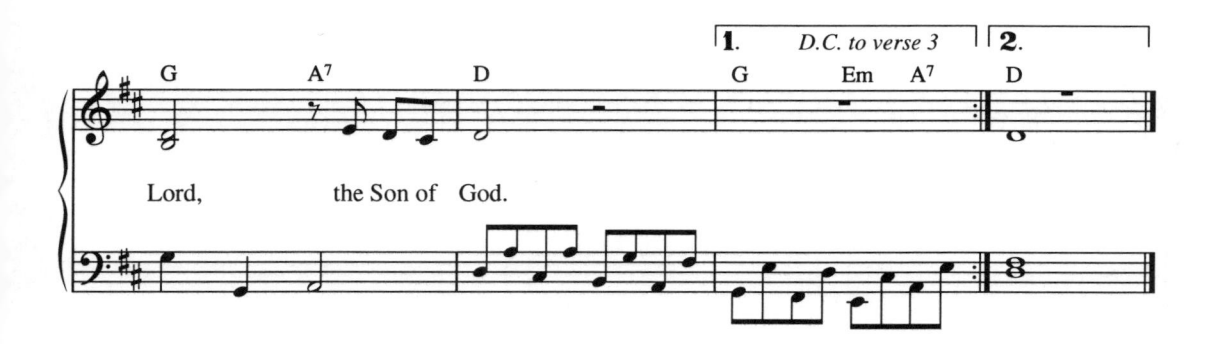

pow-er and the glo - ry of your name. The

pow-er and the glo - ry of your name. The

pow-er and the glo - ry of your name, the name of the

Lord, the Son of God.

19 This is my desire
(I give you my heart)

Reuben Morgan

This is my de-sire, to hon-our you.

Lord, with all my heart, I wor-ship you.

All I have with-in me I give you praise.

All that I a-dore is in you.

© Copyright 1995 Reuben Morgan/Hillsong Music Australia/Kingsway's Thankyou Music,
P.O. Box 75, Eastbourne, East Sussex, BN23 6NW, UK. Used by permission.

Lord I give you my heart, I give you my soul; I live for you alone. Ev-'ry breath that I take, ev-'ry mo-ment I'm a-wake, Lord, have your way in me.

20 This is the hour
(Latter rain)

Geoff Bullock

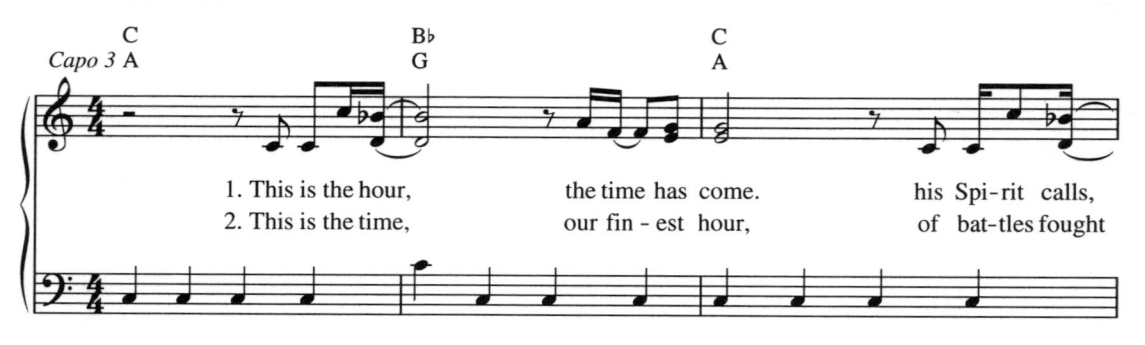

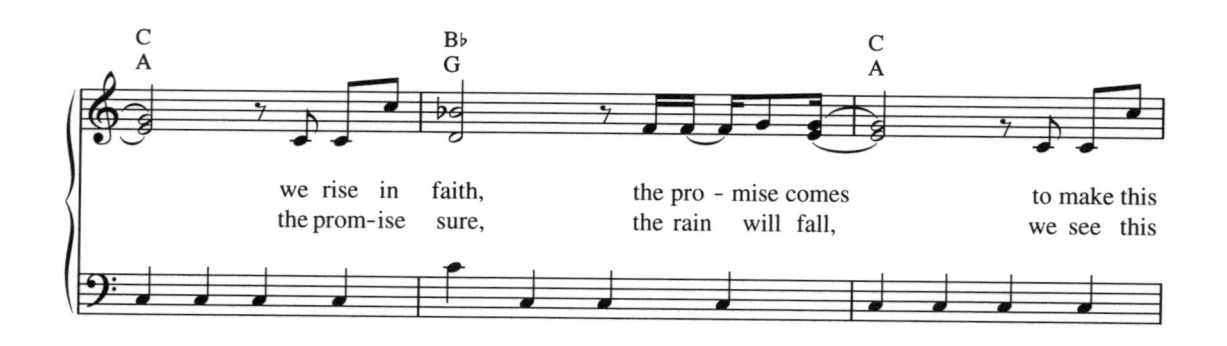

1. This is the hour, the time has come. his Spirit calls, he calls us on to make this land holy for the Lord. This is the time to seize the day, we rise in faith, the promise comes to make this

2. This is the time, our finest hour, of battles fought and vict'ries won, to make this land holy to the Lord. And from this time our future calls, the promise sure, the rain will fall, we see this

© Copyright 1992 Word/Maranatha! Music. Administered by CopyCare,
P.O. Box 77, Hailsham, East Sussex, BN27 3EF, UK. (music@copycare.com). Used by permission.

land ho-ly to the Lord.
land ho-ly to the Lord.

These are the days of the lat-ter rain, days of pow-er, days of grace.

This is the time the fire will fall,

to make this land ho - ly, to make this

land ho - ly to the Lord.

21 This love
(Now is the time)

Geoff Bullock

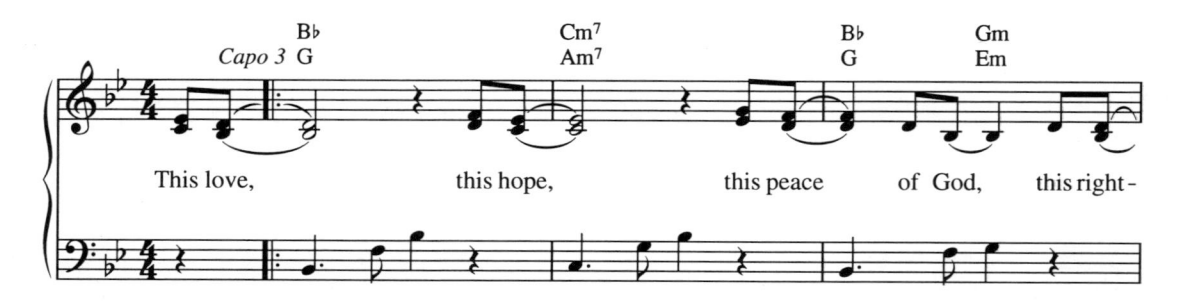

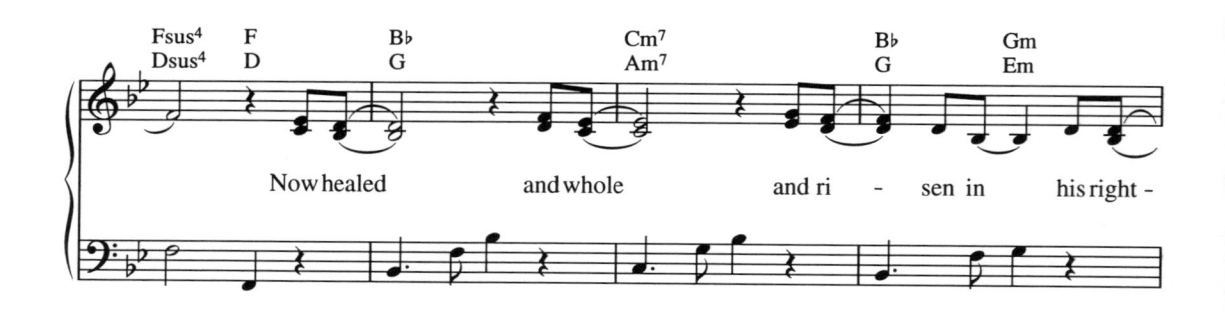

Capo 3

This love, this hope, this peace of God, this righteousness, this faith, this joy, this life, complete in me. Now healed and whole and risen in his righteousness; I live in him, he lives in me.

© Copyright 1994 Word/Maranatha! Music. Administered by CopyCare, P.O. Box 77, Hailsham, East Sussex, BN27 3EF, UK. (music@copycare.com). Used by permission.

And filled with this hope in God, re-flect-ing his glo - ry.

Now is the time to wor-ship you, now is the time to of-fer you

all of my thoughts, my dreams and plans; I lay it down.

Now is the time to live for you, now is the time I'm found in you,

now is the time your king-dom comes. This love

22. We come into your presence
(Father of creation)

Robert Eastwood

Capo 3

We come into your presence to sing a song to you, a song of praise and honour for all the things you've helped us through; you gave a life worth living, a life in love with you, and now I just love giving all my praises back to you. You're the

© Copyright 1995 Robert Eastwood/Hillsong Music Australia/Kingsway's Thankyou Music,
P.O. Box 75, Eastbourne, East Sussex, BN23 6NW, UK. Used by permission.

Father of creation, the risen Lamb of God, you're the One who walked away from the empty tomb that day; and you set your people free with love and liberty, and I can walk with you ev-'ry night and ev-'ry day. We

2. night and ev-'ry day. You're the *Last time* night and ev-'ry day.

23 We will seek your face
(Touching heaven, changing earth)

Reuben Morgan

1. We will seek your face, almighty God,
turn and pray for you to heal our land.
Father, let revival start in us,
ev'ry heart will know your kingdom come.

2. Never looking back we'll run the race,
giving you our lives we'll gain the prize.
We will take the harvest given us,
though we sow in tears, we'll reap in joy.

Chorus
Lifting up the name of the Lord, in power and in unity.

© Copyright 1997 Reuben Morgan/Hillsong Music Australia/Kingsway's Thankyou Music,
P.O. Box 75, Eastbourne, East Sussex, BN23 6NW, UK. Used by permission.

We will see the nations turn. Touch-ing hea - ven, chan - ging earth.

Touch-ing hea - ven, chang - ing earth.

Send re - vi - val,

send re - vi - val, send re - vi - val to

us. us.

24 You make your face to shine on me
(And that my soul knows very well)

Darlene Zschech and Russell Fragar

Capo 3

1. You make your face to shine on me, and that my soul knows ve-ry well. You lift me up, I'm cleansed and free, and that my soul knows ve-ry well.
2. Joy and strength each day I find, and that my soul knows ve-ry well. For-give-ness, hope, I know is mine, and that my soul knows ve-ry well.

Chorus
When moun-tains fall I'll stand by the pow-

© Copyright 1996 Darlene Zschech and Russell Fragar/Hillsong Music Australia/Kingsway's Thankyou Music, P.O. Box 75, Eastbourne, East Sussex, BN23 6NW, UK. Used by permission.

- er of your hand and in your heart of hearts I'll dwell, and that my soul knows ve - ry well.

25 Your eye is on the sparrow
(I will run to you)

Darlene Zschech

1. Your eye is on the spar-row and your hand it com-forts me. From the ends of the earth to the depths of my heart, let your mer-cy and strength be seen.

2. You call me to your pur-pose, as an-gels un-der-stand. For your glo-ry may you draw all men, as your love and grace de-mands.

Chorus
And I will run to you,

© Copyright 1996 Darlene Zschech/Hillsong Music Australia/Kingsway's Thankyou Music,
P.O. Box 75, Eastbourne, East Sussex, BN23 6NW, UK. Used by permission.

to your words of truth, not by might, not by pow-er but by the Spi-rit of God. Yes, I will run the race, 'til I see your face. Oh, let me live in the glo-ry of your grace. 2. You call